For my Grandmothers:

梁月仙

&

Eva Sounness

Against Certain Capture - Second Edition (2021).

Copyright © Miriam W. Lo (2021)

First edition published in 2004 by Five Islands Press, New Poets 10.
Second edition published by 5 Islands Press.
In 2020 5 Islands Press became an imprint of Apothecary Archive.

This book is copyright. Apart from any fair dealing for the purposes of study and research, criticism, review, or as otherwise permitted under the Copyright Act, no part may be reproduced by any process without written permission. Requests to publish work from this book should be sent to: miriamwwlo@gmail.com

Cover design: Gareth Sion Jenkins

National Library of Australia
Cataloguing-in-Publication Entry

Lo, Miriam W. 1973-
Against Certain Capture
ISBN: 978-0-6488079-7-1

Miriam W. Lo's writing has been assisted by ArtsWA.
The 2004 New Poets Publishing Program was assisted by the NSW Ministry for the Arts and by the Literature Board of the Australia Council, the Federal Government's arts funding and advisory body.

CONTENTS

Liang Yue Xian

5	Run
6	Lin Dai Yu (Self-Portrait)
8	Like the Autumn Clouds, They Are Gone
9	The Price of a Marriage
10	Do You Love Me
11	No Pretty Words
12	Truce
14	Office Photo
15	The Letter
16	Dream of Love

Eva Sounness

19	Leaving the Goldfields
20	1929
21	Saturday Night Dances
22	Keeping Her Mouth Shut
23	The War Comes Home
25	Encore
26	Between a Mother and Her Mongol Child
28	Self-Portrait
29	Farmgirl Marries
30	Don't Call Me Grandma
32	Silver

梁月仙

Run

Sometimes life
narrows down
to this
a path
cut shoulder-wide
into grass
two feet
that run
between the
rubber trees
on this
five acres

梁月仙
you hold
your name
and run
four a.m.
every morning
that doesn't
bring rain
will bring rubber

that slow
white weeping
of trees
from sharp-cut
vees into
cups which
you empty

after China
this, Kuching—
the coffeeshop
bankrupt, the
strange woman
standing beside
your father
your mother's
white-hot anger
bubbling into
sickness and
burial

here between
the trees
the running
is easy
only the
bucket grows
heavy with
latex and
counting
a cup
of white
latex for
a cup
of white
rice, some
kerosene, coffee,
cooking fat,

salt and
school fees

this path
is narrow
cut shoulder-wide
into grass
already the
heat which
dries liquid
latex to
leathery hardness
and cracks
rubber seed
into sharp
detonation
is rising
you have
two feet
so run.

Lin Dai Yu (Self-Portrait)

Lin Dai Yu: one of the main female characters
in the Chinese classic *Dream of the Red Chamber*.

Holding an egg in the palm of her hand
as her fingertips grip the brush
she writes in steady strokes
of black

> 林黛玉
> her heroine
> trapped
> in the machinations
> of family and wealth
> she loses the man she loves
> to her cousin,
> overcome by sorrow
> her body sickens and dies
> a quick death
> but her spirit—

梁月仙 lifts her brush
and presses it down again
the smooth weight of the egg in her hand,
the push of her fingers against its shell,
she will tell the story again

> 林黛玉
> her heroine
> trapped
> in the machinations
> of family and wealth
> she loses the man she loves—

to the army!
Enlisted, the fool
now gone, like her father;

> 林黛玉
> her heroine
> trapped
> in the machinations
> of family—

she will write herself free of her family,
every mark on the page
a sign of escape;

> 林黛玉
> her heroine
> trapped—

she will write
to deliver herself
from the snares of her feminine body,
from all forms of dependence,
she will write
until she can walk
through the gates of Canton University,
crack the egg
and sign
her name on the pavement
in glistening yolken gold.

Like the Autumn Clouds, They Are Gone

花样的年华,
　来如春梦不多时,
　　去似秋云无觅处。

Only the water now,
　slapping against the Vyner Brooke
　　as she stands astern and watches China

slipping away, the man with a kerosene lamp
　on the dock, growing small, swallowed up in a maze of lights
　　that recede to a dull red glow upon the horizon and then subside

into night, and so, a whole world slips away in the wash of a ship,
　the selves she could have been all laid to rest
　　in the dust of the city she has lived in.

She looks for the girl who steps out
　of a library and elbows her way
　　through a crowded street.
　　　She is gone.

Like flowers, the days of my youth—
　they came like the sweet breath of spring
　　in my dreams, like the autumn clouds
　　　they are gone where they cannot be found.

The Price of a Marriage

"A softness of the head!"
she must have thought on the nights
when he didn't come back
and she weighed the price of a marriage
against the distant rumble and crack
of mahjong tiles.

A Hakka lout for a husband
when she could have had
good Cantonese money
for silken sheets to keep her company
on nights like this.

He had spoken of love, she had laughed
at the boy with the curry-puff hairstyle,
lined him up like a card in her pack
and shuffled. Who will it be
for the prettiest girl in Kuching?
The young intellectual? The son of the rubber tycoon?

Three long years, he had spoken
beneath the clatter of coins poured out on the table,
a low sweet murmur, promising nothing more
than starlight touching the first dew of morning,
the flight of a swallow in rain,
the violet shudder of air
struck by lightning.

He still spoke of love,
on the nights he came in to stay,
to press the hard lines of her body
into frightening softness.

Do You Love Me?

She shuddered the first time she read
those words, three times this Simon Peter,
a man who had promised his life
to the one he loved,
had said, "I do not know him."

"Simon, son of John,
do you love me
more than these?"

What is love? Promises made
to be broken? The suck of soft lips
against a breast? The way a body is given?

"Simon, son of John,
do you love me?"

On the nights when all she wants
is her husband's blood
spilled out on the doorstep,
this is the question that knives her
turning her mind
between doubt and belief,
more impossible than resurrection—
to offer forgiveness.

No Pretty Words

There are no pretty words
for hunger.
Only a thin white dribble
squeezed from a cracked nipple,
the hoarse constant cry
of a baby who does not know
what it means to be full,
the sharp, angry tug
of an older child on her clothing:

妈妈，我要吃饭，妈妈！

There are no pretty words for hunger.
Only what thuds from the mouth,
flat and ugly,
like rice, fish,
sweet potato—
words to roll around in her stomach
or burn in her throat
when her husband comes home
with nothing.

She screams.
"The Japanese," he protests.
Been out gambling.

The day her breast milk dries up
there are no words at all.
She gathers her silence
and goes to the small, dark kitchen
where she grinds it together with biscuit
and mixes it with water.
This will be the word for milk
from now on.

Truce

It was as if someone said stop. Just like that. Stop.
Stop. And it did. And they all walked out in the sunlight
and blinked. Blinked. The Japanese soldiers
blinked and laid down their arms. The emperor

has surrendered. The emperor has surrendered.
Food on the table. She grants a reprieve
and the days roll on through their cycle of small events.
Laying out bread and condensed milk for breakfast.

Taking the kids to the outhouse. Another daughter. Six years
spent teaching in villages with no running water. Back in Kuching
her children point at the light bulbs in wonder. A motor car
turns down their street, they run after it, waving.

Wooden shutters push open. Metal grilles fold
and creak back. Wheels trundle
through the street below. Beneath the floorboards
a tinsmith taps on his anvil. Another morning.

She greets her mother-in-law in the kitchen.
The children, wary, take up their positions,
will it be silence today, or words
like quick bullets? She watches

her husband shift in his seat,
he will try to outrun her:
Politics, Business Interests, Elections;
try to regain lost ground

by stealth, by impressive achievement: City Councillor.
Chairman of the Chinese School Teacher's Union.
Assistant Minister. The man revered
for knowing his electorate by name.

It's all the same. More big dinners.
More late nights out. More parades to attend.
She beats a quick retreat to the bedroom. Complains
of indigestion. Complains when he comes home past twelve.

She clings to routine, walks the same path
to the market each day, closing her eyes to the people
who whisper and wave. Down Carpenter Street.
Up to Gambier Road. She buys bread

from the same stall. She fingers the dry ikan bilis
almost bought yesterday and then lets it fall.
The butcher slaps pork on the counter.
As they always have, the vegetable sellers call—

"Sweet cucumber! Fresh fern leaf from up-country!"
Above her head, the swallows wheel and return.
Chicken blood runs in the gutters. She stares.
Last night he brought soup to her bedside. Double-boiled chicken.

Office Photo

Could happiness consist in sitting still?
He leans his arm on a shining table top.
The chipboard back of her chair reassures her.
Tethered to objects, she sits and smiles at the camera.

Tethered to objects, she sits and smiles.
Behind her back the washbasin tap is dripping.
Could happiness consist in sitting still?
Her husband shuts the filing cabinet door.

He leans his arm on the shining table top.
A black telephone squats at right angles to his elbow.
His eyes are puffy from last night's celebrations.
The chipboard back of her chair reassures her.

The chipboard back of her chair reassures.
Her white leather handbag is perched on her lap.
Tethered to objects, she sits and smiles.
The camera clicks, the phone begins to ring.

Her husband picks it up and starts to talk.
He presses his elbows into the shining table.
She turns her head to see the window grille.
Could happiness consist in sitting still?

The grille is styled in heart-shaped curlicues.
Her own heart flutters sightly, comes to rest,
tethered to objects. The chipboard veneer is thin.
Outside the window, night waits to come in.

He leans his arm on the shining table.
He smiles at the chipboard back of her chair.

The Letter

How it sits in his hands.

"Who's it from?"
Her son looks away.
"Su-san."
Su-san. A girl's name.
An Australian girl is writing to her son.
The coffeeshop patrons grow quiet.
Fat sizzles in the restaurant's woks, upstairs.
Traffic roars round the corner.

Questions,
as if he is suddenly a stranger,
as if he has come from a far-away place,
sat down in strange clothes, demanding a coffee.

Someone strange has come in and sat down in their coffee-shop.
There! Her breath in the words of the letter.
A glimpse of the handwriting—
round, neat letters.
A faint outline of a person is starting to form.

His mother thinks of how words
flow out of a body and carry a ghost
of fingers, a face, a heart.
She thinks of the words that have etched themselves
on the walls of her life: *I surrender*,
We are at war; the words that weigh heavily
on her tongue as she stands and watches
the face of her son: *I love you, come home.*
Come Home.

But she cannot hold him, how quickly he slips from her gaze
to those words on the page
that are taking him away
to a place she has no name for.

Dreaming of Love

In the morning, it lights up the ceiling and whispers her name.
She wakes and watches it flutter across her face.

She turns on her side, slowly,
and touches the floorboards, they throb beneath her,
warm, the room is alive, the curtains flash pink and gold,
the walls spin white and the door trembles.

Trembles.

Ah Hiang pushes it open.
Breakfast. Rice porridge. Eat, eat.
The spoon slips from her hand. She is dreaming—
the servants bathe her and carry her downstairs.

In the dayroom, she asks for a video.
Cantonese lovers pledge eternal faithfulness
or vow revenge, tearful families
betray star-crossed lovers or weep
at reunions. She smiles and dabs
her wet cheeks with pink tissues on cue.

It is true. She turns off the light and drifts
back over her life. What he said, what she did,
what he did, what she said, but love—
is hovering above her head,
she feels its cool breath on her scalp,
the rustle of wings at her shoulder.

Love takes her hand. They walk back
over her life. They consider each wound, she fingers
each scab and lets go of scratching.

Love pulls back the curtains
and finds the clenched dagger
she's held in her heart since the day she was born.

She surrenders the dagger.

Love wipes the blade clean.

She opens her eyes.
Someone has been planting flowers—
a climbing rose pushes its way through her TV screen,
the walls are covered with jasmine,
a peach tree, laden with fruit, has sprung up through the floor.

Someone has opened the door,
small children she does not know
scramble through her house,
chickens cluck and nest on the sofas,
a mousedeer nudges her knee with its nose.

She tries to get up.
She calls for her daughter.
"This cat," she says, "did you buy it for me?"
"Your father," she says, "he was here just now,
did you offer him something to drink?"
"No," her daughter replies
and looks at her strangely.

The angels beside her say "Peace, Peace."
She hears the knock on the door
and asks for some milk.
She puts her hand over her heart,
where it aches,
and slips back into the dream of love.

Eva Sounness

Leaving the Goldfields

Eva sits on the train. She is watching the crowd
  at the station, the precise expression of faces,
    the way a man crinkles his brow as he blows unshed tears

into his safe handkerchief. They are leaving,
  leaving the dust of Kalgoorlie, the red saltbush plains,
    the jostle of mining equipment against the horizon,

the chimneys, the skeleton structures of tall poppet heads,
  the way the earth swallows men up and spits them out
    with a faint trace of gold in their sweat.

Eva sits on the train. She is memorising
  the colour of Kalgoorlie dust. She is calling to mind
    the names of her friends, she is sketching

a house in the distance that leans, small and empty
  against the wind. She is tracing the contours of shopfronts
    and running her hand over faces to capture the shape of a nose.

She is taking it with her. Packing it up in a bag
  like a painting, a series of clay figurines,
    a charcoal sketch she returns to, over and over,
    smudging out lines and shading in features,
  trying to bring back the shape of a roof, the way
two lips purse and open to say farewell.

1929

1s11d for a yard of rayon—
Eva stares at the pinks and greens
in the draper's window,
That's up from last month.
She turns and walks up York Street.
Tram fares are up, price of bread,
price of mutton. "Paper, Miss?"
Eva smiles, "No thank you."
"Leaving Results today, Miss?"
"No thank you."

Eva has seen the results,
all fifteen letters of her name
stamped in black type on the bursary list.
"Well?" says her mother,
"Just missed a distinction in French."
Eva's mouth holds the twist of a smile.
She has seen her father,
white from exertion,
stumble up steps,
hand clutched at his chest.
She knows the word
that hangs in the air
between them
angina
and knows
that hope
is a thing to be swallowed,
to hold in the belly
until it turns sour.

Stomach knotted in place,
Eva walks up York Street
pausing to note
what the shop windows tell her today
about the cost of living.

Saturday Night Dances

There is a type of man at the Saturday dances
who generally stands in the corner discussing the cricket
or football. Mt Barker, Saturday night. Cliff glances

across the room. The boys hold forth on the wickets
that just keep falling, bodyline bowling, the Don—
his next strategy. Something makes Clifford forget

his description of Bradman's style. Is it the song
that they're playing, or, the woman who stands there waiting
to be asked? Eva is glad for someone to lean on,

she notes that his arms are steady, although his dancing
leaves something to be desired. As they move, she weights
his soberness against bandy legs, his shuffling

two-step, the smell of the farm on his collar. She sways.
Above their heads the song of the fiddle plays.

Keeping Her Mouth Shut

It is an act
Eva becomes practiced in—
pressing her lips together,
clamping her teeth down on words
that rise from her belly like bile:
Stop telling me what to do and
Mind your own business.
She becomes adept at moulding her mouth
into innocuous smiles—
the proper response to her mother-in-law
who lifts an eyebrow to say:
You haven't polished the silver
and frowns, to remind her:
You're not a farmer's daughter.

No, not a farmer's daughter.
Eva lifts her head to the window
scanning the dark line of trees against the horizon,
this could be hostile country,
the orchards sinister with the drop of fruit,
the rippling stretches of field concealing fences,
the trembling fault-lines of ownership, belonging, property.
Propriety. Eva arches her eyebrows in return,
swivels her elbows, puts on her most polite
and mocking smile
and slowly pours some tea.

The War Comes Home

When the war begins
Eva is feeding her first daughter, Robin, oat porridge
boiled soft for her infant mouth which drops to an O
at the sight of the spoon, the small pink tongue expectant.
Kim, her son, is running around in the yard
rounding up chooks and shouting at sleepy dogs,
pretending to be a farmer.

Somewhere faraway
a place called Austria is annexed, Poland collapses,
Jews are garrotted and pinioned in ghettos.
With the usual burst of wattle and birdsong
spring arrives in the South-West corner
of Western Australia, which is, Robert Menzies declares,
also at war.

In China, the blood has been running
for months, years, is dripping off crusted walls
in tight alleyways, congealing in gutters, and all they hear
in Mt Barker is the crackling cut-and-dried
news on the radio: *No Real Cause for Alarm* and
Business as Usual and Eva is pregnant
with twins.

Canberra bickers. Two heads and a tangle
of limbs press themselves against Eva's taut abdomen.
Menzies resigns, Arthur Fadden stretches himself
across forty days, two independents take a short walk
to John Curtin's government. Labor. "Good,"
says Eva, "no more crawling to London." Cliff scowls
and rustles the newspaper.

Closer to home
there is rustling through jungle. Impregnable:
word like a fortress falling apart, cracking up into syllables:
did not think the Japs would get here so fast. Footsteps at the door
carry the prospect of carnage. The children rush in
suddenly soft and vulnerable as newborns. Eva cradles the twins.
Disaster is one panicked moment: *What if I lost them?*

Losing is for other people's children. Here,
the war is a headache that lasts six years,
tightening sometimes into a deep sense of unease—
a little like standing in the kitchen
waiting for the baby to cry itself out.
Pain that belongs to somebody else.

Encore

Look again,
these are the years of her womanhood
in full stride, hips set firm,
knees articulating smoothly,
calf muscles clenching, releasing,
in swift, irrevocable footsteps.

Observe the sweep of her arms
as she moves between washing lines:
poised, perfect as a dancer, pegs clipping down
with the precision of pincers;
the arch of her back over mangles and tubs
has the grace of a fountain
fluid and tumbling.

Take note of her hands:
blunt-nailed, thick-fingered, deft
with a paring knife, swift with a needle, tender
over the peas, slicing through air
to smack a small offender.

Hear her sing out the names of her children:
"Kim, Robin, Helen and Margaret, Garry, Lynley, Gay, Richard,
Susan."

Watch her with eyes
that will hold her, here, forever,
in these years of her dancing,
fingers travelling over the whites and blacks
of the upright piano, play us a song
that will stay with us, Eva,
sing to us in your clear, unwavering voice.

Between a Mother and Her Mongol Child

Mongolism: Currently known as Down or Down's Syndrome, also called Trisomy 21. The disorder is the result of a genetic anomaly in which an extra chromosome presents on pair 21.

I) stopheart

                                                              wrench fuse stop spark
                                              short copper wire short short

        switch click   switch switch   click
    bodystrapped   fingertips   won't come on
       stairwinding   skitter up feetfirst afraid of the dark

                          wrench
                  guttering fusebox

     sleepdream small house sparkling sawdust
hands thrusting pears into fencepoles   washhouse alight
   switch woman runs apple foot over stone cottages
        everlastings strike   goldwater
           curly haired   witchwoman   scratches
               painting   swims   scholar
              drowns in saltwater
          climbs into the sharp white cot
            picks up the blue baby
                and drops

spanner
pass me the butter knife

        cut   over
        open   the box
        connect the wiring   start
        the stop   heart   startstop
        the   stopheart

"When I knew she had to come home ... something clicked."

II) Rewind

Eva opens her arms. She takes the flat face,
the slant eyes, the delicate body,
the skin that curves up into cheeks,
the haphazard wisps of blond hair—

> "It was Angela's first smile that gave me a glimmer of hope. She was so cute and sweet and seemed to want to hold on fast to me. It took some time before the Mongol became a child and I became interested in her progress ... One day, when she was about three, I was holding her and she said: 'Your hands are warm. Your face is warm, love me too?' And in my mind I composed this little poem and I have never told it to anyone but you:
>
> Your hands are warm.
> Your face is warm.
> I love your warm face,
> I love your warm hands.
> Love me too?
>
> Yes, my darling,
> Indeed I do.
> Best in all the world I love you too.
> No love song this,
> Sealed with passionate kiss,
> But soft words spoken
> Sweet and mild,
> Between a mother
> And her Mongol child."

Something clicked into place. The clockwork
of her heart, perhaps, turning again, as her arms
come to life and reach out to pick up this child—
Angela.

Self Portrait

She begins with faces:
the jut of a chin, the way a nose splits
a face into two rough halves, the soft kohl
of eyelashes, the crooked lift of a brow—
she takes up charcoal and sketches,
scattering family and friends over scraps of paper,
leaving profiles on napkins and notebooks.

One morning, she finds herself caught.
Charcoal stick angled in hand,
Eva hesitates—
sounding out silence
she waits for an echo, an answer:
memory murmurs, faintly,
the sound of a pencil, scratching,
the view from a train;
stronger, something replies,
seizing her fingers—
she sweeps in arcs of black across the page.

A face emerges:
eyes that hold secrets swirled
in the iris, pupils opening
pinprick out into darkness,
a mouth with lips pressed together,
a nose pushing forward,
suggesting a hook,
skin that is starting to pucker
around the eyes,
crease-lines on the forehead,
beneath the chin,
a neck that is starting to drop.

She adds a peaked black hat for effect.

Farmgirl Marries

BRIGHT-EYED SUSIE DROPS BOMBSHELL.
There, at the dining room table, she lets it fall,
news of the decade, they sit in silence
a moment, her mother begins to talk—
SHOCK NEWS DOES NOT GO DOWN WELL.

PARENTS DISAPPROVE.
"Over my dead body," says Eva as Cliff
clears his throat and removes himself from the table.
They wait for the slam of the door.
SUSIE MAKES MOVE.

GIRL RUNS CRYING FROM MOTHER.
Eva tries to make her see reason:
"It's wrong to marry someone from a different race!"
Susie runs down the road to her brother's place.
SOBBING SUSIE MAKES PHONECALL TO CHINESE LOVER.

"MARRIAGE CAN WAIT TWO YEARS"
says Cliff, extracting a promise
from sobbing Susie. He'll work the miracle yet,
he'll cure his girl of this strange malaise.
NEWS CONFIRMS PARENT'S WORST FEARS.

SUSIE TO MARRY IN DECEMBER.
Can't keep her word. Cliff swears
he'll not attend the wedding. Eva says,
"They're very determined," and picks up a pen.
CHINESE FIANCE RECEIVES NASTY LETTER.

DETERMINED COUPLE THWART MOTHER'S PLAN.
"Marriage is difficult enough," writes Eva,
"without your interference," thinks Susie.
"We'll sign the papers in advance," says Danny.
FARMGIRL MARRIES CHINAMAN.

Don't Call Me Grandma

"Don't call me Grandma
when I'm in here
call me old witch Eva"—
      that always stopped us
on the threshold,
words whistling out into breath,
we'd watch
a moment longer,
she'd move
between the lumps of clay,
a half-formed pot on a wheel,
hair catching light
through a dusty window—
"Grandma,"
we'd say,
"Don't call me Grandma
when I'm in here!"

"Old witch Eva,
can I come in?
Can I make something too?"
Magic words,
we'd pass that magic line
where house crossed into shed
and grandmas into witches.
Pressing our own cold lumps of clay
into clumsy teapots and lopsided animals,
we'd watch her shift
across the room, her woolly hair
bunned up or streaming down,
a sudden glance, a little stare,
she still looked like Grandma
but you couldn't be sure—
Was that a broomstick in the corner?
An owl perched on her chair?

She'd whisk around and lift her arms
to make us shriek,
then settle to her work—
the rhythmic squeak
of a potter's wheel,
the whisper of slurry
on hands throwing clay
and behind her back,
the night-bird, startled from sleep,
stretches up on its chair
and begins to beat its wings.

Silver

Eva rises, drawing her years about her—
a cloak of thick and silvering hair
that hangs past her shoulders.

Slowly, she turns on her feet,
her dance adagio, her gestures
stately, deliberate.

Still capable of quick rhythm,
she spins to surprise a small child—
old age is not stillness,

but a gathering in. They move towards her,
the grandchildren, hands outstretched
to grasp a body in motion,

a body still drawing in warmth to itself
to breathe it out, luminescent
in clay figurines, in the paint that glitters

beady in a numbat's eye, into the sun
as it strikes the Stirling Ranges—
late afternoon light, throwing each peak,

each leaf, into soft-edged focus,
as if a farewell was forming against the horizon,
as if a farewell could fall like dusk from her lips.

Chronology

Liang Yue Xian

1918 Yue Xian born in Kuching, Malaysia.
1929 Yue Xian and family return from China.
1938 Japanese approach Canton. Yue Xian and sisters return to Kuching again, relinquishing prospects of further education.
1941 Yue Xian marries Lo Foot Kee. Japanese take Kuching.
1959 Foot Kee quits teaching to go into politics.
1961 Foot Kee quits politics to go into business.
1962 Yue Xian's son goes to Australia on a Colombo Plan scholarship.
1970 Yue Xian's son marries.
1979 Foot Kee dies.
1985 Yue Xian is baptised.

Eva Tamar Sounness

1912 Eva born in Boulder, Western Australia.
1926 Eva's family move to Albany.
1935 Eva marries Cliff.
1955 Eva spends six months hospitalised in Perth for nervous breakdown following birth of tenth child.
1960 Eva and family move from Mt Barker to the Stirling Ranges.
1970 Eva's ninth child marries a Chinese student.
1986 Eva and Cliff retire to Albany.

Acknowledgements

My grandmothers: for allowing me to plunder their lives.

My parents, in-laws and extended family: for their considerable support.

My immediate family: for believing in my work, even when I have wavered.

All the poets in Western Australia: for keeping the flame alive. (Especially Dennis Haskell and John Kinsella, who have kept prodding me.)

Sheridan Institute in Perth: it is such a privilege to teach creative writing here.

The community of creatives at the Akimbo workshops, especially my tribe of lions: I would never have attempted a second edition without your advice and encouragement.

The first edition of *Against Certain Capture* was published by Five Islands Press in 2004 as part of the New Poets 10 series. For this, I owe a debt of gratitude to Ron Pretty. I am grateful also to Gareth Jenkins of Apothecary Archive for publishing this second edition.

Poems in this collection have appeared (sometimes as different versions) in *Westerly*, *Hecate*, *The Journal of Australian Studies*, *My Cat Cannot Have Friends in Australia*, *Blue Dog*, *Windchimes*, *The Best Australian Poems*, *Contemporary Asian Australian Poets*, and *To Gather Your Leaving*. This collection as a whole won the 2004 West Australian Premier's Book Award for poetry.

The Whadjuk Noongar people: whose unceded boodja I live and work upon.

God: the first Creative. Let there be light.

www.ingramcontent.com/pod-product-compliance
Lightning Source LLC
Chambersburg PA
CBHW020913020526
44107CB00075B/1808